What others are saying about this book . . .

"Reads like the Rosetta Stone into the often elusive realm of prosperity—crafted with impact, yet elegant simplicity. These 101 Keys remind us all of our enormous potential AND how to achieve even greater prosperity."

– Art Burleigh
Double Diamond Executive

"First he was an avid student of the simple Truths. Then he became a Master of them. Now he is a Mentor Extraordinaire. Any definition of prosperous living would have to include the name of Randy Gage. His "101 Keys to Your Prosperity" should be required reading for a high school diploma and is a must-read (and re-read) for anyone who seeks happiness and abundance."

– Vic Johnson
AsAManThinketh.net

Randy Gage's "101 Keys To Your Prosperity" breaks down everything you need to know to increase your prosperity—from someone who has actually done what they're teaching. Best of all it is presented in a way that isn't loaded down with a lot of excess fluff! This book is packed from the first page to the last with ideas that you can begin applying immediately.

– Josh Hinds
GetMotivation.com

"From the Introduction all the way through #101, Randy hits the nail square on the head . . . with a sledgehammer! This mini-book is absolute Gage-filled excellence!"

– Bryan Hall

Randy Gage's unique and brilliant insights make this book a must read, a must read 3x a year! Don't just get this book, GRAB this book because your next level life awaits you!

– Mike Litman
Autho ~~~ **with Millionaires**

101 Keys To Your
Prosperity

"Insights on health, happiness and abundance in your life"

By Randy Gage

Gage, Randy.
   101 keys to your prosperity / by Randy Gage.
   — 1st ed.
   p. cm.
   One-hundred-one keys to your prosperity
   "Insights on health, happiness and abundance in your life."
   LCCN 2003102880
   ISBN 0971557845

   1. Success—Psychological aspects. 2. Critical
   thinking. 3. Visualization. 4. Self-actualization
   (Psychology) I. Title. II. Title: One-hundred-one
   keys to your prosperity

   BF637.S8G34 2003   158.1
                               QBI33-1268

"101 Keys To Your Prosperity" is book one in a five-book series on Prosperity.

101 Keys to Your Prosperity

Accept Your Abundance! Why You are supposed to be Wealthy

37 Secrets About Prosperity

The 7 Spiritual Laws of Prosperity and How to Manifest Them in Your Life

Prosperity Mind: How to Harness the Power of Thought

Published by:
Prime Concepts Publishing
A Division of Prime Concepts Group, Inc.
1807 S. Eisenhower Street
Wichita, Kansas 67209-2810 USA

Order Information:
To order more copies of this book, or to receive a complete catalog of other products by Randy Gage, contact:

Prime Concepts Group, Inc.
1-800-946-7804 or (316) 942-1111
or purchase online at:
www.RandyGage.com
www.Prosperity-Insights.com

This book is dedicated to my
Mastermind Council.

Introduction

I don't know how to say this without sounding melodramatic, so let me be melodramatic. What you are holding in your hands now has the power to transform your life in beautiful, wondrous, and spiritual ways. This book is not large, but it is substantial. It encapsulates 101 keys to manifesting the prosperity in your life. Really.

As you will discover, poverty, lack, and limitation are not an absence of things or opportunities. Poverty, like its corresponding opposite prosperity, is simply a state of mind. It is with that thought that I bring these 101 insights to your attention.

I believe that you were born to be wealthy. And I believe the way to manifest that, is by expanding your consciousness and accepting what is rightfully yours. Also know that I say that not because it's "new-agey", trendy, or it was revealed to me by visitors from another outer space.

I'm a very rational, logical guy, who has spent the better part of 15 years studying the universal laws that prosperity is based on. When you live your life in accordance with these laws, you manifest prosperity and abundance in your life. When the laws are broken, you get the lesson repeated.

I wrote this book in order that you may claim your birthright, and accept the abundance that is yours. The next step is yours . . .

Randy Gage
Hollywood, Florida
March 2003

Believe in your good before
you see it.

1

Stop taking financial advice
from broke people.

2

Vividly image what you
desire in your mind.

3

Your wealth will grow only
as fast as you do.

4

5

Seek mentors who have done what you desire to do.

6

Seek mentors who have become what you desire to be.

7

Plant seeds for your future prosperity.

8

If you have old debts you never paid back-pay them forward.

Tip that extra five percent.

9

Never affirm lack.

10

Health, love, happiness
and money are infinite.

11

Operate your life by the
philosophy of trading value
for value.

12

13

Buy some fresh flowers for someone special. Like yourself.

14

You must create a vacuum for good.

15

The universe cannot put good into your hand until you let go of what you are holding in it.

16

Ask for what you think you want, but know that you will get what you really want.

The fastest way to become wealthy is to find ways to provide value to others.

17

The most powerful prosperity tool is wisdom.

18

The words you speak reflect the prosperity consciousness you possess.

19

True prosperity only comes to those who seek it.

20

21

Wisdom is more important than, money, jewels and precious metals, because wisdom will get you all of those things.

22

Increase your wisdom and you will always manifest a corresponding increase in wealth.

23

True health comes from being comfortable in your own skin.

24

Prosperity is your birthright and your natural condition.

Prosperity is in the ethers all around you. There is no place on earth that prosperity is not.

25

Man can manifest prosperity from the ethers by the power of ideas, vision, and imagination.

26

When you discover your true assignment, prosperity will find you.

27

When you are willing to release being a victim, you open the path to become a victor.

28

29 If you want people to feel sorry for you, you will continually manifest situations that foster that.

30 Once you have a clear vision, you bend the universe to your will.

31 When you throw revenge out, love will walk in.

32 Miracles are not accidents. And they happen daily.

Your income and prosperity will be the average of your five closest friends.

33

You cannot borrow your way to prosperity.

34

Debt is a prison best left as soon as possible.

35

If you cannot forgive others, you cannot accept abundance.

36

37 If you cannot forgive yourself, you cannot accept abundance.

38 The universe will give you your next assignment when you are overqualified for this one.

39 Setbacks are stepping stones to becoming the person you need to be-to get the things you desire.

40 Faith is more powerful than bricks, mortar, or steel. It is what draws your prosperity from the storehouse.

The universe can only do for you, what can be done through you.

41

You change your circumstances when you change your habits.

42

You change your habits when you change your beliefs.

43

You change your beliefs when you allow yourself the luxury of critical thinking.

44

45 Words are powerful prosperity tools.

46 Prescriptions, operations and crutches are for temporary healing. True health comes from reverting to your natural state.

47 You would be hard pressed to find someone more prosperous than a three-year-old with a box of crayons and a coloring book.

48 The universe makes the light available to you, but you must still turn on the light switch.

If you want abundance in your life, you must live in accordance with spiritual laws.

49

Gossiping about others creates a negative prosperity debt.

50

Set aside daily time for self-development.

51

Tithe 10% back to the source of your spiritual nourishment.

52

53 Tithe on the gross, not the net.

54 Give your tithes lovingly, joyfully and gratefully.

55 The universe will always get its tithe. Better to do if of your own choice.

56 Be willing to give away something you possess, to receive something you desire.

Logic will analyze, but only faith will take action.

57

You must be willing to fight for your dreams, against the negativity of the herd.

58

Be the number one investor in your dream.

59

Spend more on your development than you do at the coffee shop.

60

61

Build your own dream instead of borrowing the dreams of others.

62

You don't have to push money out to let God or the Universe in.

63

True success in an endeavor requires an obsession.

64

The best way to raise your self-confidence is proper planning.

Only acknowledge your limitations for the purpose of overcoming them.

65

Don't share your problems with people who can't make them go away.

66

If your dreams are not bold, daring and imaginative, they are simply fodder for your enemies to use against you.

67

If you don't invest in you, why should anyone else?

68

69

Your dream needs to be as big as you are.

70

Announcing your dream will recruit the people who will help you, and expose your enemies.

71

To embolden yourself, associate with bold people.

72

Send forth an anonymous seed offering to someone who needs it.

You are a spiritual being having a human experience, not the other way around.

73

Teach people how to fish. When they want the all-you-can-eat Fish Fry, direct them to another table.

74

Find five people that were in a bookstore this week, and make them your close friends.

75

Prosperous people drive clean cars, live in clean houses, and dress well.

76

77 Washing a rental car, or making your bed in a hotel room is only affirming your great value to yourself.

78 Poverty causes people to lie, cheat, steal and even kill. There is nothing spiritual about poverty.

79 If you don't pay more now for a pair of shoes than you used to spend on a car, your prosperity consciousness needs work.

80 Discipline provides freedom.

Write a movie script of your vision. Involve all of your senses.

81

Bills are simply invoices for blessings you've already received.

82

Create a "Dream Board" and keep it where you will pass it every day.

83

Don't focus on coupons, discounts and negotiating. Pay a fair price joyfully.

84

85

Zealously analyze the shows, publications, and movies you are exposed to for the subliminal programming they give you.

86

Prosperity has almost nothing to do with opportunities, chance, luck—or even training, education, or skill. It is your consciousness and beliefs that create your prosperity.

Some rich people are sick, bitter and lonely. They are not prosperous. By the same token, if you are healthy, spiritually grounded, and have a great marriage, but struggle to pay your credit cards each month—you are certainly not prosperous either. Prosperity is all encompassing.

87

You are being programmed all day, every day. You can't stop it, but you can determine if the programming is positive or negative.

88

89 Successful people start a project expecting success.

90 Surround yourself with people who dream bigger than you do.

91 Fear of success holds back more people than fear of failure ever did.

92 Poverty is not a lack of things; it is a mindset.

Prosperity is not an abundance of things; it is a mindset.

93

The slave and the oppressor are co-creators in ignorance and lack.

94

Your mind is an instrument for poverty or prosperity.

95

You can't out give the universe.

96

97 Understanding that selfishness is a virtue is the first step to abundance and prosperity.

98 The best thing you can do for the poor, starving and downtrodden, is to not be one of them.

99 When you get negative people out of your life, negative things stop happening to you.

100 Take a little step closer to your dream each day.

Your dream has never
been closer than it is at
this exact instant.

101

Final Thoughts . . .

If this book has blessed you, please multiply the vision of a prosperous world. This book is available in quantity discounts, in order that you may share with your network, associates, family, or study group. Practice the circulation law of prosperity!

-RG

Quantity Price List for *101 Keys to Your Prosperity*

1 – 9 books	$7.00 each
10 – 99 books	6.00 each
100 – 499 books	5.00 each
500 – 999 books	4.00 each
1,000 + books	3.00 each

For shipping costs and quantities over 5,000 books, please contact the publisher.

Other Prosperity books by Randy Gage in this series

Accept Your Abundance!

37 Secrets About Prosperity

The 7 Spiritual Laws of Prosperity and How to Manifest Them in Your Life

Prosperity Mind: How to Harness the Power of Thought

**All books are available online at
www.Prosperity-Insights.com**

About Randy Gage

For more than 15 years, Randy Gage has been helping people transform self-limiting beliefs into self-fulfilling breakthroughs to achieve their dreams. Randy's story of rising from a jail cell as a teen, to a self-made millionaire, has inspired millions around the world.

This compelling journey of triumph over fear, self-doubt, and addiction, uniquely qualifies him as an undisputed expert in the arena of peak performance and extraordinary human achievement. His story and the way he shares it, demonstrate the true power of the mind over outside circumstances.

Randy Gage is a modern-day explorer in the field of body-mind development and personal growth. He is the author of many best-selling albums including, *Dynamic Development* and *Prosperity* and is the director of www.BreakthroughU.com.

People from around the world interact and receive personal coaching from Randy through "Breakthrough U," his online coaching and success program. As Dean of BreakthroughU.com, Randy provides insight into how to overcome fear, doubt and self-sabotage to reach success and achieve the highest level of human potential.

For more resources and to subscribe to Randy's free ezine newsletters, visit www.RandyGage.com.

101 Keys to Your Prosperity

"Insights on health, happiness and abundance in your life."

You are meant to be healthy, happy and prosperous. Once you recognize and accept this, it is simply a case of learning the principles that abundance is based on.

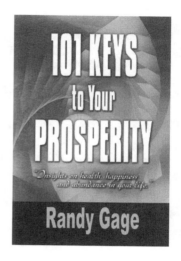

In this insightful book, Randy Gage reveals 101 keys to manifesting that prosperity in your own life. You will move from lack consciousness to living in the light of true abundance. You'll discover:

- What creates prosperity consciousness;
- The universal laws that govern prosperity;
- Why you should embrace critical thinking;
- The secret of creating a vacuum for good; and,
- What it takes to manifest prosperity on the physical plane.

Order the print book or downloadable eBook online at www.Prosperity-Insights.com

Quantity pricing for paperback book:

1–9 books	$7.00 each
10–99 books	$6.00 each
100–499 books	$5.00 each
500–999 books	$4.00 each
1,000 + books	$3.00 each

Order Online at **www.Prosperity-Insights.com**
or call 1-800-432-4243 or (316) 942-1111

Accept Your Abundance!
Why You are Supposed to Be Wealthy

"Claim the Prosperity That is Your Birthright."

Do you believe that it is somehow spiritual to be poor? One reading of this fascinating book will dissuade you of that belief fast. You'll understand that you are meant to be healthy, happy and wealthy.

Prosperity guru Randy Gage cuts through the religious dogmas to reveal why becoming rich is your spiritual destiny. You'll discover:

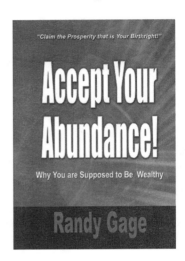

- Why poverty is a sin;
- What may be keeping you from your prosperity;
- Why being wealthy is your natural state;
- The difference between the way rich and poor people think; and,
- How to attract and accept your true abundance!

Order the print book or downloadable eBook online at www.Prosperity-Insights.com

Quantity pricing for paperback book:

1–9 books	$7.00 each
10–99 books	$6.00 each
100–499 books	$5.00 each
500–999 books	$4.00 each
1,000 + books	$3.00 each

37 Secrets About Prosperity

"A revealing look at how you manifest wealth."

In this landmark book, prosperity guru Randy Gage unveils 37 little-known insights into the science of prosperity. Gage breaks it down into simple, understandable explanations, so you can apply the information in your life immediately to create your own prosperity. He reveals how he went from a dishwasher in a pancake house to a self-made multi-millionaire.

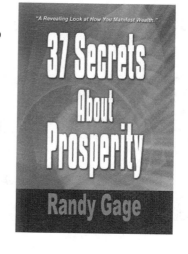

You'll learn:

- Why most people remain poor;
- How the rich leverage their prosperity;
- Why you should emulate certain business models;
- What separates broke, sick and unhappy people from the rich, healthy and happy ones; and,
- How you can manifest prosperity in all areas of your life.

Order the print book or downloadable eBook online at www.Prosperity-Insights.com

Quantity pricing for paperback book:

1–9 books	$7.00 each
10–99 books	$6.00 each
100–499 books	$5.00 each
500–999 books	$4.00 each
1,000 + books	$3.00 each

Prosperity Mind!
How to Harness the Power of Thought
"Brilliant Insights on health, happiness and abundance in your life."

Since "Think and Grow Rich," people have been fascinated with the power of the mind to accomplish great things. Now a recognized expert in human potential cracks the code on how you program yourself for prosperity!

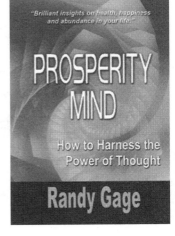

In this breakthrough book, prosperity guru Randy Gage reveals how you can actually program your subconscious mind to move from lack consciousness to prosperity thought. In it, you'll discover:

- How to identify self-limiting beliefs that hold you back;
- The 5 common expressions you probably use every day, which program you for failure on a subconscious level;
- How to practice the "vacuum law" of prosperity to attract good in your life;
- Imaging techniques to manifest things you want; and,
- How you can actually program your own subconscious mind for riches!

Order the print book or downloadable eBook online at www.Prosperity-Insights.com

Quantity pricing for paperback book:

1–9 books	$7.00 each
10–99 books	$6.00 each
100–499 books	$5.00 each
500–999 books	$4.00 each
1,000 + books	$3.00 each

The 7 Spiritual Laws of Prosperity

"Live your life by the universal laws that govern health, happiness and abundance."

It is your birthright to be healthy, happy and prosperous. Accept this truth and it's simply a case of learning and living by the 7 Spiritual Laws that govern abundance.

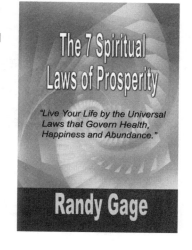

In this breakthrough and insightful book, Randy Gage reveals the secrets behind harnessing these laws to manifest your own prosperity. You'll learn about each of these Prosperity Laws and discover how to:

- Create a vacuum for good;
- Use imaging to get what you want;
- Find and keep your perfect soul mate;
- Use creativity to get the bills paid; and,
- Attract money, health and harmony to your life.

Order the print book or downloadable eBook online at www.Prosperity-Insights.com

Quantity pricing for paperback book:

1–9 books	$7.00 each
10–99 books	$6.00 each
100–499 books	$5.00 each
500–999 books	$4.00 each
1,000 + books	$3.00 each

The Prosperity Series
by Randy Gage

You are meant to be healthy, happy and prosperous. Once you recognize and accept this, it is simply a case of learning the principles that abundance is based on.

In this insightful series, you will move from lack consciousness to living in the light of true abundance.

Randy Gage reveals . . .

- What creates prosperity consciousness;
- The universal laws that govern prosperity;
- Why you should embrace critical thinking;
- The secret of creating a vacuum for good;
- What it takes to manifest prosperity on the physical plane; and,
- Why you are supposed to be wealthy.

Get all five books now and start living a life of abundance!

Order Prosperity Series by Randy Gage online:
www.Prosperity-Insights.com

The Prosperity Series, 5 print books $30
The Prosperity Series, 5 eBooks $20
The Prosperity Series, all 5 print books and eBooks
Combination Special $47

Prosperity:
How to Apply Spiritual Laws to Create Health, Wealth and Abundance in Your Life by Randy Gage

This album will help you uncover the subconscious "lack" programming you have that is holding you back. Then, you'll replace it with prosperity consciousness to manifest money, health, great relationships, happiness, and strong spiritual harmony.

True prosperity comes from understanding and living by the spiritual laws that govern our world. This album takes you through each of the Seven Spiritual Laws that govern prosperity—and shows you how to apply them. You will discover the ancient secrets to manifest prosperity in your own life.

You'll discover:

- Why you're supposed to be rich;
- The secrets of optimum health;
- How to get out of debt;
- The Seven Spiritual Laws you must live by;
- Your special powers for prosperity; and,
- How to image—then manifest—boundless, limitless prosperity.

This album will take you on a journey of spiritual enlightenment. You'll learn the practical applications so you can manifest prosperity in your life NOW! You'll learn about faith, the principle of attraction, and even how to use creativity to get the bills paid! This is the most specific, detailed and comprehensive album ever produced on how to become prosperous. **Don't you need it now?**

Prosperity: 8 CD album #A28CD $107
Prosperity: 8 audio-tape album #A28 $97

Dynamic Development
Achieve Your True Potential with the Dynamic Development Series
by Randy Gage

Do you live a life of joy—or simply get through the week? Can you communicate well with your family and co-workers, or do you struggle to be heard? Are you in open, honest and loving relationships, or do you hide behind a mask? <u>How much more can you earn, learn, love and accomplish</u>? *If you want to break out of self-imposed limitations and break through to your true potential—the **Dynamic Development Series** is the perfect resource for you.*

Instantly hailed when it was released as the ultimate self-development resource, this is a two-year program to nurture your personal growth and achieve your innate greatness. Each month you will receive an audiotape from human achievement expert Randy Gage with a lesson, and some "homework" to complete that month.

It's a continuing journey on your path of personal development. Each month will bring you on an in-depth study in some area of human achievement, whether body, mind or soul. You'll discover new truths about yourself and uncover old ones. You'll desire more, obtain more, and accomplish more . . . by becoming more.

Dynamic Development, Volume 1, 12 audio-tapes
#V2 $147

Dynamic Development, Volume2, 12 audio-tapes
V4 $147

BEST DEAL! Both Dynamic Development Volumes,
24 audio-tapes #V2V4S $247

Crafting Your Vision

Twelve success experts share their secrets to success . . .

As soon as this 12 audio-tape album was released, it was hailed as one of the greatest self-development tools since *Think and Grow Rich!* I t gets to the real root cause of success or failure—the vision you create for yourself.

It's pleasing to your ego to assume your prosperity is not growing because of outside factors and other circumstances. **But the truth is—you are reaping the results of the vision you created!**

Your suffering, frustration or failure to reach goals is the result of a neutral or negative vision—just as the blessings in your life are the results of a positive vision. This is an immutable, unshakable universal law. Living the lifestyle of your dreams begins with crafting the vision of where you want to go. For without a clear, compelling vision you simply cannot achieve what you're truly capable of. And there simply is no better resource to help you create an empowering vision for yourself than this amazing resource.

You'll learn how to craft your personal vision, how to design a vision big enough to encompass the visions of your people, and the steps to take on a daily basis to bring your vision to reality. You'll hear 12 complete programs on vision—recorded live—from 12 of the foremost experts on direct selling, recruiting and marketing.

This breakthrough album includes talks by:

Richard Brooke	Michael S. Clouse	Rita Davenport
John Milton Fogg	Matthew Freese	Randy Gage
Lisa Jimenez, M.Ed.	John Kalench	John David Mann
Jan Ruhe	Tom Schreiter	Tom Welch

When you finish, you'll really know how to craft and manifest the vision of where you want to go. Make sure this resource is in your personal development library. **Get it today!**

Crafting Your Vision: 12 audio-tape album #A30 $97

Get Randy Gage As

The only ongoing education program specifically designed for your success! Get personal, individualized success coaching from **Randy Gage**. Join Randy as he helps you expand your vision, shatter self-doubt, and reach your true success potential. Breakthrough U is your opportunity to have Randy as your personal success coach—mentoring you through the mindset, consciousness, and daily actions necessary to reach the success you are capable of.

Initiate Level

This is level one of an amazing journey of self-discovery. Each day you will receive a "Daily Awakening" e-mail message filled with mind-expanding exercises and success lessons to teach you how to think like ultra-successful people think. In addition to these "mind aerobics," you'll receive marketing tips, prosperity secrets and just general success information on how to make it to the top.

You will also have access to the members-only forum on the site so that you can network with other success-minded individuals, and get an invitation to attend Randy's Breakthrough U Success Events.

This is priced inexpensively and is for the beginning success seeker. If you've faced adversity, are deeply in debt, maxed out on your credit cards, or simply starting the journey—this is the program for you. Randy created this level so that those who are down and out— but committed to getting "up and in" —have a vehicle to do so. It's a program to change your consciousness, one day at a time.

Now, if you are further along the path, and serious about reaching higher levels of success—you're ready to advance to...

Alchemist Level

Alchemy, if you'll remember, is the medieval philosophy of transmutation: converting base metals to gold. This is the level for you if you're seeking a transmutation in your life: converting base thoughts and desires into the thinking and actions that produce rich and prosperous outcomes.

(continued on the next page)

Your Personal Coach!

Like the Initiate Level, you will receive the Daily Awakening messages, access to the members-only forum, and an invitation to Randy's Success Convention. You will also receive:

- The "Alchemy Transmutation Kit" (with intro lesson, CDs and binder);
- A subscription to the monthly lessons;
- Access to the monthly online video seminars;
- Monthly Tele-seminars
- Two Personalized Consultations

Now, if you're serious as a heart attack about success, and want to get even more individualized and personal coaching . . . you might want to consider the pinnacle level:

Mastermind Council

This is Randy's "inner circle" of select consulting clients, business partners, and colleagues. They receive a package of benefits so lucrative, that it's never been offered anywhere before. Membership in the **Mastermind Council** gives you a chance to get the most personalized help and guidance from Randy individually—as well as interacting with some of the brightest entrepreneurial minds on the planet.

In addition to the same benefits as the Alchemist, you will also receive:

- Ten Personalized Consultations;
- The chance to participate in twelve live Mastermind Conference Calls a year;
- Members-only Council Updates; and,
- The chance to participate in the Mastermind Retreats each year.

For complete details go to:
www.BreakthroughU.com

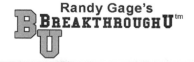

Randy Gage's
BREAKTHROUGHU™

The Midas Mentality:
Expecting and Accepting Your Abundance

This program is the first resource of its kind, ever developed in the world. It will transform you from lack and limitation programming to prosperity consciousness. For 31 days, Randy Gage will work with you, helping you go through the same transformation that he did. He will help you peel away limiting beliefs and replace them with beliefs that serve you and he will help you identify fears and conquer them.

And level upon level, he will guide you in a metamorphosis of your thought process—from how sick, unhappy and broke people think—to the way healthy, happy, rich people do.

30 Audio CDs, 2 DVDs, Study Guide & Randy Jr. CDRom

It is a multi-media format, scientifically developed to literally change the way you think. You will create new neural pathways in your brain, develop your critical thinking skills, and foster whole brain synchronicity between the two hemispheres of your brain.

You will develop the multi-millionaire's mindset, which is the first—and most critical—step to becoming open.

On day one, you'll watch the DVD entitled, "The Science of Manifesting Prosperity." Then you'll load the CD-ROM into your computer. This will cause the "Randy Jr" character to pop up on your computer screen once each day, giving you one of his 101 keys to prosperity.

Then on the next day, you'll start the first of 30 daily lessons on audio CD. You listen to each lesson, then go to your workbook and complete the day's task. On average, this will take you from 45 minutes an hour per day. Do only one lesson each day, to ensure that it "sets," and you are at a different consciousness when you start the next day's lesson.

Following the thirty CDs and workbook lessons, you then watch the final DVD, "Putting Your Prosperity in Place." Of course the "Randy Jr." character will keep popping up everyday, to keep your thoughts on track.

Trust me when I tell you that you will be thinking entirely different than when you started. You will have the mindset of a multi-millionaire, the single most important step to becoming one. You see, you can't be treated for prosperity; you can only be open to receiving it. By the time you finish this program, you will be. Really.

The Midas Mentality–30 audio CDs, 2 DVDs, Study Guide & Randy Jr. CDRom $997

Order Online at **www.ProsperityUniverse.com**
or call 1-800-432-4243 or (316) 942-1111

Randy Gage's Recommended Resources	Price	Qty	Total
Prosperity by Randy Gage Select: ¨ audiotapes or ¨ CD's	$97 (tapes) $107 (CDs)		
The Midas Mentality 30 day prosperity program	$997		
Dynamic Development Series Volume One by Randy Gage	$147		
Crafting Your Vision 12 audiotape album	$97		
Prosperity Series 5 books	$30		
101 Keys to Your Prosperity book	$7		
The 7 Spiritual Laws of Prosperity book	$7		
Prosperity Mind! book	$7		
Accept Your Abundance! book	$7		
37 Secrets About Prosperity book	$7		

United Parcel Shipping Table			Subtotal

United Parcel Shipping Table

Order Total	2-Day	Ground
$50.00 or under	$11.60	$5.50
$50.01-$250.00	$13.20	$6.00
$250.01-over	$16.20	$7.00

Subtotal

$\_\_\_\_\_$

For Alaska, Hawaii, and Canada - regular shipping cost, and add 10%. For foreign and overseas orders, figure the total of your order, plus the regular shipping cost, and add 20%

Shipping (see chart)

$\_\_\_\_\_$

Terms: 60-day money back guarantee! Contact us within 60 days of your invoice date if, for any reason, you're not 100% satisfied with any product you've received from us. Product must be in re-sellable condition. Customer Service: 1-800-946-7804 or (316) 942-1111

$\_\_\_\_\_$
TOTAL

PAYMENT TYPE: ¨ **Visa**   ¨ **MC**   ¨ **AMEX**   ¨ **Discover**   **or**
¨ **Cash**   ¨ **Check**

Please print clearly
Credit Card # _ _ _ _ _ _ _ _ _ _ _ _ _ _ _ _

Expires: (MM/YY) ____/____ Signature:_____

Full Name:

Address: Apt./Suite#

City: **State:**   **Zip:**   **Country:**

Phone: **Email:**

Ordering & Customer Service: Prime Concepts Group Inc.
1807 S. Eisenhower St. • Wichita, Kansas 67209-2810 USA
1-800-432-4243 or (316) 942-1111 • Fax: (316) 942-5313
www.ProsperityUniverse.com